Table of Contents

INTRODUCTION

Hey, teens! Your parents may give you some cash toward the things you want to buy, but you may feel better if you could earn and save money to put towards your goals. This is why it's important to know how to handle personal finances and why we're giving you financial tips for teens. While you may need to learn geography and geometry to get your high school diploma, some important life skills aren't always taught in school. Budgeting is a real-life skill that you can practice every day to set yourself up for financial   success.

14 TIPS ON BUDGETING FOR TEENS TO START GROWING YOUR MONEY YOUNG.

1. Know Your Income

The first step to budgeting is knowing how much money you make. Whether you have an income from a part-time job or just have a monthly allowance for helping around the house, you should total up the amount of money you make each month. Whatever that number is, use it as a guide for your spending and saving. If that total varies from month to month, air on the safe side and stick to the smaller amount.

2. Create Budget Categories

The next tip is to create your budget categories. When creating categories, keep in mind two main ones: saving and spending. Under these two categories, list out the different expenses that you'll be putting your money toward. You can see an example of budget categories below.

Saving

Savings account

College fund

Short- and long-term purchases (e.g., a car or laptop)

Retirement savings

Spending

Necessary expenses:

Gas money

Phone bill

Lunch money

Other expenses:

Gym membership

Subscription services

Other food/treats (coffee, fast food, frozen yogurt, etc.)

Clothes and accessories

Grooming and beauty services

Entertainment and activities

Most teens don't have to worry about paying for housing or utilities, so don't include those if someone takes care of them for you. If you do contribute to those, though, feel free to include them as necessary spending expenses.

3. Pick a Budgeting Strategy

Once you have a list of all your categories, it's time to figure out how much money to allot for each one. You can do this using a variety of budgeting methods. Learn more about a few different strategies below and choose the one that works best for you.

"Pay Yourself First" method: Paying yourself first means that you immediately put a certain amount or percentage of your income into savings. Whatever money is left over can be spent however you choose.

Zero-based budgeting: Want to account for every dollar in your budget? This method operates off of the idea that when you subtract your expenses from your income, the result is zero. Estimate the cost of each budget category and divvy up your income until you hit zero, using those estimates as a guide.

50/30/20 rule: This rule budgets your money based on the following percentages: 50 percent for necessary expenses, 30 percent for other expenses, and 20 percent for savings. These percentages can be altered to fit your needs, and if you don't have many expenses, you may want to contribute the larger percentage toward savings.

4. Save First, Spend Later

Now that you've decided on a way to budget, it's smart to always contribute to savings before you start spending. If you start spending before you save, there's a chance that you might blow your budget one month and not have anything left over to save. By prioritizing the act of saving, you practice discipline with your money and make it easier to stick to the budget you planned in the first place.

5. Set Goals

Having goals for your money is a great way to motivate yourself to stick to your budget. Maybe you're saving up for your very own car or a trip with friends. Whatever your goals are, if you maintain your budget and keep up good saving and spending habits, you'll achieve them in no time.

6. Track Your Habits

Another helpful budgeting tip is to start tracking your spending habits. Use this printable habit tracker to monitor and reflect on your weekly spending. By tracking your habits, you can figure out if you can make some realistic lifestyle swaps to save more. For example, if you find yourself splurging on iced coffee multiple times a week, try out a more budget-friendly alternative like making it at home and putting it in a to-go cup. A simple modification to a big habit may just free up a sizable chunk of change in your budget.7. Adjust Your Budget

If you find that your budget isn't working for you, know that you can change it to fit your needs. For example, if you're consistently overspending on something necessary like gas, adjust your budget to fit that need better. On the other hand, if you've stopped driving as much, feel free to allocate your gas funds somewhere else, like toward savings. If you're overspending on something that's more of a want, like clothes or entertainment, figure out ways to curb your spending. An alternative to this is to think about reworking other non-essential expense categories to free up more funds. Once you have the availability in your budget, you can feel guilt-free about spending on what makes you happy.

8. Learn From Your Mistakes

Mistakes happen, but what's important is what you learn from them. Did you fall short of your savings goal and now have to skip out on a fun activity or settle for a cheaper alternative? Reflect on why you fell short of your goal, and think about how you can do better next time. Good spending and saving habits come with practice, so remember to use the feeling of not meeting your goal to do better next time.

9. Earn More With a Side Hustle

If you find that you'd prefer to have more wiggle room with your budget, look into increasing your income with a side hustle. There are many ways for teens to make extra cash from the comfort of your own home. Try putting your interests or talents to work with some of these side hustles:

Start a podcast

Pet sit or walk dogs

Sell baked goods

Tutor others in a skill or subject

10. Be a Spending Minimalist

When it comes to spending, less is more. That is, you'll have more money if you spend less. Take on a minimalist lifestyle and mindset with these tips:

Try a capsule wardrobe and only invest in select, high-quality clothes

Give life to old items by saving money and shopping secondhand

Find ways to repurpose and appreciate what you already have

11. Don't Give In To Peer Pressure

Life as a teen comes with many pressures. Whether it's keeping up with current fashion trends or grabbing a bite to eat with friends, you may be tempted to overspend often. Don't feel bad about not having the latest accessories or asking your friends to hang out at the park instead of dining out. True friends are happy to hang out with you regardless of what you're wearing or where you are.

12. Seek Out Help

When it comes to budgeting as a teen, remember to seek out help when you need it. You're still learning about many different parts of life, and it's all right to not have all the answers. If you have questions, get advice from your parents or other financial role models. Do your own research and read books by financial experts or listen to podcasts online to dive into more complicated topics like investing.

13. Find a Way to Have Fun

Technology and social media are other resources that make budgeting fun and easy. Use an app like Mint to budget right from your phone or check out videos online to learn more about financial terms. Read on to the next section for more advice on budgeting for teens from your favorite social media stars.

14. Follow Money-Minded Influencers

A great way to level up your money mindset is through social media. Watch these TikTok stars break down financial concepts and offer tips in short video snippets.

8 FINANCIAL TIPS FOR YOUNG ADULTS

1. Pay With Cash, Not Credit

Exercise patience and self-control with your finances. If you wait and save money for what you need, you will pay with cash or a debit card to deduct money directly from your checking account and avoid using a credit card. A credit card is a loan that accumulates interest unless you can afford to pay off the balance in full every month. Credit cards can help you build a good credit score but use them for emergencies only.

2. Educate Yourself

Take charge of your financial future and read a few basic books on personal finance. Once armed with knowledge, don't let anyone take you off track, whether a significant other who encourages you to waste money or friends who plan expensive trips and events you can't afford. Research professionals like financial planners, mortgage lenders, or accountants before utilizing their services.

3. Learn To Budget

Once you've read a few personal finance books, you will understand two rules. Never let your expenses exceed your income, and watch where your money goes. The best way to do this is by budgeting and creating a personal spending plan to track the money coming in and going out. Tracking expenses, like your expensive morning coffee, can provide a valuable wake-up call. Small changes in your everyday expenses are under your control and can impact your financial situation. Keeping monthly expenses, like rent, as low as possible can save you money over time and put you in a position to invest in your own home sooner than later.

4. Start an Emergency Fund

A mantra in personal finance is "pay yourself first," which means saving money for emergencies and your future. This simple practice keeps you out of trouble financially and helps you sleep better at night. The tightest budget should put some money into an emergency fund every month. Once you get into the habit of saving money, you will stop treating savings as optional and start treating it as a required monthly expense. Many accounts offer the power of compound interest, such as a high-yield savings account, short-term certificate of deposit (CD), or money market account.

5. Save for Retirement Now

No matter how young you are, plan for your retirement now. With the power of compound interest, when you start saving in your 20s, you will earn interest not only on the principal you deposit but also on the interest you earn over time, and you will have what you need to retire someday. Company-sponsored retirement plans are a great choice. Not only do you get to put in pretax dollars, but many companies will also match part of your contribution, which is free money. Contribution limits tend to be higher for 401(k)s than for individual retirement accounts (IRAs), but both are one step closer to financial health. If you invest

$200 a month, averaging a positive return of 9% annually over 40 years, you will save $856,214 for retirement.

6. Monitor Your Taxes

When a company offers you a starting salary, calculate whether that salary after taxes meets your financial needs and savings goals. Many online calculators help you see your after-tax salary, such as PaycheckCity.com, and chart your gross pay (total earnings) and net pay (earnings after taxes and other deductions or take-home pay). In 2023, an annual salary of $35,000 in New York netted $28,461 after federal and state taxes, or about $2,372 per month. In the U.S., low-income earners are taxed at a lower rate than higher-income earners—the higher your salary, the higher the tax rate. A salary increase from $35,000 to $41,000 a year looks like an extra $6,000 per year or $500 per month, but the tax rate will be higher, so it will only give you $4,463, or $372 per month.

7. Guard Your Health

If you're uninsured, don't wait to apply for health insurance. If employed, your employer may offer health insurance, including high-deductible health plans that save on premiums and qualify you for a Health Savings Account (HSA). If you're under the age of 26, you may be able to stay on your parent's health insurance, an option that has been allowed since the 2010 passage of the Affordable Care Act (ACA).

If you need to buy insurance, investigate the federal and state plans offered by the Health Insurance Marketplace of the ACA. Look at quotes from different insurance providers to find the lowest rates. Research all your options to see if you qualify for a subsidy based on your income.

8. Protect Your Wealth

If you rent, get renter's insurance to protect the contents of your home from loss due to burglary or fire. Read the policy carefully to see what's covered and what isn't. Disability insurance protects your ability to earn an income by providing you with a steady income if you are unable to work for an extended period due to illness or injury. If you want help managing your money, find a fee-only financial planner to provide unbiased advice. Unlike a commission-based financial advisor, who earns money when you sign up with the investments their company markets, a fee-only planner can provide advice in your best interest.

PERSONAL SPENDING PLAN: WHAT IT MEANS, HOW IT WORKS

A spending plan is an informal document used to determine the cash flow of an individual or household. A personal spending plan, similar to one's budget, helps outline where income is earned and where expenses are incurred. When paired with a financial goals worksheet, the personal spending plan can be used to create a roadmap for monitoring spending, as well as helping determine the most appropriate methods for saving. A personal spending plan is a modification of a personal budget, indicating sources of income along with outflows, identifying patterns of spending, and highlighting needs vs. wants.

Instead of viewing the plan as restrictive, think about the things it allows you to buy and how you will spend your money.

Adopting a personal spending plan as part of an overall financial plan is a good way to take control of your spending, live within your means, and, ultimately, reach your financial goals.

Understanding Personal Spending Plans

A personal spending plan is a more individualized and flexible take on the traditional budget. While many people may be familiar with their sources of income, such as a salary from a job, fewer know the patterns that may be associated with where that income is spent. A family may want to integrate a household spending plan in order to track what each member of the family spends and find ways to save or budget funds. The personal spending plan is often more detailed than a standard budget because it requires more information about each item. By documenting and categorizing all sources of spending, individuals and families can better understand whether funds are being spent on items that detract from their ability to save for and reach their financial goals.

Making Financial Goals with a Spending Plan

Financial goals are integral to making a personal spending plan work. Financial goals, such as saving money for a vacation, or buying a new home, help individuals determine how much money should be diverted from living expenses into savings and investing. It is not necessary to use a financial planner to make a spending plan, it can be as simple as using a shareable spreadsheet or online money tracker. Reporting all spending is necessary to keep an accurate and detailed account of each category of spending, like groceries, school-related fees, or entertainment. Some experts recommend that families or single-person households spend a month or two recording all their expenditures before embarking on a spending plan. In doing so, it is likely possible to make realistic financial goals, when it comes time to implement a spending plan.

Create Your Personal Spending Plan

Nearly everyone wishes to have more money at some point. That said, all but the wealthiest among us are essentially living on a fixed income based on our labor income each week or month. In other words, you bring in a certain amount of money each pay period, and when it's gone, it's gone. Accepting that reality is the key to living a happier, wealthier life. Keep in mind that your creditors don't work for free, so spending money that you don't have is also incredibly expensive. Fortunately, getting your finances on track isn't that difficult. While there are spreadsheets and software programs designed to make the budgeting process faster and easier, all you really need is a piece of paper, a pencil, and the desire to live within (or even below) your means. The example below will help you get started.

Monthly Expenses   Cost

Rent   ?

Insurance   ?

Transportation ?

Utilities   ?

Food   ?

Entertainment ?

Clothes   ?

Emergency Fund   ?

As a general rule, you should also plan to set aside enough money to cover at least three months' worth of your expenses in case of an emergency. Once that money is put away, you won't need to rely on your credit cards should you lose your job or experience unforeseen expenses. Like every other recurring item in your personal spending plan, the emergency fund is something you fund one month at a time until you reach your goal.

What Is a Budget?

The term budget refers to an estimation of revenue and expenses over a specified future period of time and is usually compiled and re-evaluated on a periodic basis. Budgets can be made for any entity that wants to spend money, including governments and businesses, along with people and households at any income level. To manage your monthly expenses, prepare for life's unpredictable events, and be able to afford big-ticket items without going into debt, budgeting is important. Keeping track of how much you earn and spend doesn't have to be drudgery, doesn't require you to be good at math, and doesn't mean you can't buy the things you want. It just means that you'll know where your money goes, and you'll have greater control over your finances.

Understanding Budgeting

A budget is a microeconomic concept that shows the trade-off made when one good is exchanged for another. In terms of the bottom line—or the end result of this trade-off—a surplus budget means profits are anticipated, a balanced budget means revenues are expected to equal expenses, and a deficit budget means expenses will exceed revenues.

How to Budget in 7 Steps

The specifics of your budget will depend on your personal financial situation and goals. In most cases, though, the steps for creating a budget are the same. You can make a budget by following seven simple steps.

Add up your total income. This should include all sources, such as a paycheck, tips, Social Security, disability, alimony, or investment income.

Track your spending. Spend a month keeping track of everything you spend, whether you pay with a credit card or cash, to find what your real expenses are. Be sure to include automatic payments, subscriptions, and utilities.

Set financial goals. Do you want to save money? Pay off debt? Stop overspending? Decide on realistic goals. Remember, you can adjust these over time. Pick the most pressing goals, such as paying off debt or creating an emergency fund, first.

Calculate mandatory expenses. These are expenses you must pay each month, such as rent, insurance premiums, taxes, childcare, or your cell phone bill. Subtract these from your total income.

Identify debt payments. If you are paying off debt, such as student loans or a credit card bill, find the minimum payment for each debt. Subtract that from your income as well.

Make a spending plan. The amount of income you have left is what you can spend on discretionary expenses. These can include your goals, such as debt payment or savings. It should also include things like groceries, entertainment, gas, or surprise expenses. Give every dollar a job, based on your goals and what you discovered when you tracked your spending.

Adjust each month. Each month, look at your spending and goals, Reevaluate and adjust where you assign your discretionary spending. A flexible budget will help you avoid overspending.

Corporate Budgets

Budgets are an integral part of running any business efficiently and effectively.

Budget Development Process
The process begins by establishing assumptions for the upcoming budget period. These assumptions are related to projected sales trends, cost trends, and the overall economic outlook of the market, industry, or sector. Specific factors affecting potential expenses are addressed and monitored. The budget is published in a packet that outlines the standards and procedures used to develop it, including the assumptions about the markets, key relationships with

vendors that provide discounts, and explanations of how certain calculations were made.

The sales budget is often the first to be developed, as subsequent expense budgets cannot be established without knowing future cash flows. Budgets are developed for all the different subsidiaries, divisions, and departments within an organization. For a manufacturer, a separate budget is often developed for direct materials, labor, and overhead. All budgets get rolled up into the master budget, which also includes budgeted financial statements, forecasts of cash inflows and outflows, and an overall financing plan. At a corporation, the top management reviews the budget and submits it for approval to the board of directors.

Static vs. Flexible Budgets
There are two major types of budgets: static budgets and flexible budgets. A static budget remains unchanged over the life of the budget. Regardless of changes that occur during the budgeting period, all accounts and figures originally calculated remain the same. A flexible budget has a relational value to certain variables. The dollar

amounts listed on a flexible budget change based on sales levels, production levels, or other external economic factors. Both types of budgets are useful for management. A static budget evaluates the effectiveness of the original budgeting process, while a flexible budget provides deeper insight into business operations.

The importance of budgeting cannot be understated. A budget, also known as cash flow, is arguably more important than the actual cash that you have in your bank and investment accounts. Your cash flow is what allows you to pay for everything (or not). Without knowing your cash flow, you could be putting yourself into a bad financial situation and not even know it. You can only get by without knowing your cash flow for so long before you get into financial trouble, so make the time you know the flow of your cash. Budgeting should be something that everyone does, regardless of their financial situation.

Personal Budgets

Individuals and families can have budgets, too. Creating and using a budget is not just for those who need to closely monitor their cash flows from month to month because money is tight. Almost everyone can benefit from budgeting—even people with large paychecks and plenty of money in the bank. Budgeting is a wonderful tool for managing your finances, but many people think it's not for them. Below is a list of budget myths—the erroneous logic that stops people from keeping track of their finances and allocating money in the best way.

1. I Don't Need to Budget

Having a handle on your monthly income and expenses allows you to make sure your hard-earned money is being put to its highest and best purpose. For those who enjoy an income that covers all bills with money left over, a budget can help maximize savings and investments. If one's monthly expenses typically consume the lion's share of net income, any budget should focus on identifying and classifying all the expenses that occur during the month, quarter, and year. And for people whose cash flow is tight, it can be crucial for identifying expenses that could be reduced or cut, and minimizing any wasteful interest being paid on credit cards or other debt.

2. I'm Not Good at Math

Thanks to budgeting software, you don't have to be good at math; you simply have to be able to follow instructions. Many of these programs are free and legitimate. If you know how to use spreadsheet software, you can make your own ledger. It's as simple as creating one column for your income, another column for your expenses, and then keeping a running tab on the difference between the two.

3. My Job Is Secure

No one's job is truly safe. If you work for a corporation, being laid off due to downsizing or a takeover always is a possibility. If you work for a small company, it could die with its owner, be bought out, or just fold. You should always be prepared for a job loss by having at least three months' worth of living expenses in the bank. It's easier to accumulate this financial cushion if you know the amount you're bringing in and spending each month, which can be monitored with a budget.

4. Unemployment Insurance Will Tide Me Over

Unemployment compensation is not a sure thing. Let's say a bad situation at work leaves you with no choice but to quit your job. Unless you can prove constructive discharge (that is, you were virtually forced to resign), your departure will be considered voluntary, making you ineligible for unemployment insurance. Besides, the benefits may fall well short of the wages you're used to: for most states, they average between $300 and $500 per week.

5. I Don't Want to Deprive Myself

Budgeting is not synonymous with spending as little money as possible or making yourself feel guilty about every purchase. The aim of budgeting is to make sure you're able to save a little each month, ideally at least 10% of your income, or at the very least, to make sure that you aren't spending more than you earn. Unless you're on a very tight budget, you should be able to buy baseball tickets and go out to eat. Tracking your expenses does not change the amount of money you have available to spend every month; it just tells you where that money is going.

6. I Don't Want Anything Big

If you don't have any major savings goals (upsizing your living situation, starting your own business, etc.), it's hard to drum up the motivation to stash away extra cash each month. However, your situation and your attitudes likely will change over time. Let's say you and your partner live in New York City in a small one-bedroom apartment and things are going fine for the both of you until your family dynamic changes. For instance, you may have a child or an in-law who comes to stay with you indefinitely, which means you'll probably need (and want) more room to accommodate the new addition. If you don't save up for anything big, you may not be able to afford this change in your living situation later on down the road.

7. I Won't Qualify for Student Financial Aid

Yes, the catch-22 of student financial aid is that the more money you have, the less aid you'll be eligible for. That's enough to make anyone wonder if it isn't better to just spend it all and have no savings in order to qualify for the maximum amount of grants and loans. But that catch mainly applies to earned income. Whether you are an adult student going back to school or the parent of a student headed to college, the Free Application for Federal Student Aid (FAFSA) form (used for Stafford Loans, Perkins Loans, or Pell Grants), does not require you to report the value of your primary residence (if you own a home) or the value of your retirement accounts.

So if you want to save money without compromising your financial aid eligibility, you can do so by using your savings to buy a house, prepay your mortgage, or contribute more money to your retirement accounts. The savings you put into these assets can still be accessed if you face an emergency, but you won't be penalized for it. Even if you employ all the available legal strategies to maximize your financial aid eligibility, you still won't always qualify for as much aid as you need, so it's not a bad idea to have your own source of funds to make up for any shortfall.

8. I'm Debt-Free

Good for you! But being debt-free without any savings won't pay your bills in an emergency. A zero balance can quickly become a negative balance if you don't have a safety net.

9. I Always Get a Raise or Tax Refund

It's never a good idea to count on unpredictable sources of income. This may be the year your company may not have enough money to give you a raise or as much of a raise as you'd hoped for. The same is true of bonus money. Tax refunds are more reliable, but this depends in part on how good you are at calculating your own tax liability. Some people know how to figure how much they'll get in a refund (or how much they will owe) as well as how to adjust this figure through changes in payroll withholding throughout the year. However, changes in tax deductions, IRS regulations, or other life events can mean a nasty surprise on your tax return.

10. I Just Don't Have the Discipline

If you're still not convinced that budgeting is for you, here's a way to protect yourself from your own spending habits. Set up an automatic transfer from your checking account to a savings account you won't see (i.e., at a different bank), scheduled to happen right after you get paid. If you are saving for retirement, you may have the option of contributing a set amount regularly to a 401(k) or other retirement savings plan. This way, you can pay yourself first, have enough money for the transfer, and pay yourself the same predetermined amount that you know will help you meet your savings goals.

11. It's a Luxury When I Barely Have Enough for the Essentials

Sometimes budgeting just isn't a priority because you may have too many other things on your plate. But there are certain government programs that can help you manage your household expenses. For instance, the Supplemental Nutrition Assistance Program (SNAP) helps recipients of all income levels work with their food budgets to make their benefits go further.

First Steps in Building a Budget
In general, traditional budgeting starts with tracking expenses, eliminating debt, and once the budget is balanced, building an emergency fund. But to speed up the process, you could start by building a partial emergency fund. This emergency fund acts as a buffer as the rest of the budget is put in place and should replace the use of credit cards for emergency situations. The key is to build the fund at regular intervals, consistently devoting a certain percentage

of each paycheck toward it, and if possible, putting in whatever you can spare on top. This will get you to think about your spending, too.

What's an Emergency?

You should only use the emergency money for true emergencies. For instance, if you lose your job and need to pay for expenses, you could tap into your rainy day fund until you join the workforce again. You can also use this money if you have an unexpected medical emergency that arises..You would save money if you used your emergency fund to eliminate credit card debt, but the purpose of the fund is to prevent you from having to use your credit card for paying for unexpected expenses. With a proper emergency fund, you will not need your credit card to keep you afloat when something goes wrong.

Downsize and Substitute

Now that you have a buffer between you and high-interest debt, it is time to start the process of downsizing. The more space you can create between your expenses and your income, the more income you will have to pay down debt and invest. This can be a process of substitution as much as elimination. For example, cancel any recurring subscriptions that you don't regularly use or need. Use half of the money you save to invest or pay off outstanding debts, and save the other half to begin building a home gym in your basement. Although eliminating expenses entirely is the fastest way to a solid budget, substitution tends to have more lasting effects. So:

Consider shopping with friends and family so you can split the cost, especially if you buy in bulk.

Carpooling or taking public transport is another great way to cut down on your transportation costs.

People often cut too deep and end up making a budget that they can't keep because it feels like they are giving up everything. Substitution, in contrast, keeps the basics while cutting down costs.

Find New Sources of Income

Why isn't this the first step? If you simply increase your income without a budget to handle the extra cash properly, the gains tend to slip through the cracks and vanish. Once you have your budget in place and have more money coming in than going out (along with the buffer of an emergency fund), you can start investing to create more income. It is better to have no debt before you begin investing. If you are young, however, the rewards of investing in higher-risk, high-return vehicles like stocks can outweigh most low-interest debt over time.

How to Build a Complete Budget

Now that you know the steps it takes to build a budget, you'll need to know how to build it. We've outlined the basics of how to craft a comprehensive budget below. Some of the information listed here has already been discussed. But it helps to reiterate it.

Calculate your total monthly income. This includes any wages, salaries, tips, benefits, and any other money that you get on a regular, monthly basis.

Determine your normal monthly expenses. Some of these are predictable, which makes them easier to work, especially if they don't change every month. Think of your mortgage or rent, utility payments, transportation costs, and other similar expenses. Some may fluctuate each month like your food or clothing costs. In these cases, it's always a good idea to err. onside the caution and budget a little higher. Be sure to include your debt, as well, such as loans and credit card payments.

Plan for any extras, including spending money in case you want to dine out, order takeout, see a movie, or do any other activity.

Note down any amount that you'll set aside for savings if that's in your plan.

Now that you have these figures, calculate your plan and write it out. A budget doesn't (and can't) work if you don't put it in writing. If you see it, you'll have more incentive to stick to it. You may have to do some juggling, especially in the initial few months. This means adjusting here and there so you stay within your planned budget. But once you've passed this hurdle, it should be fairly problem-free going forward. If you can, though, keep your receipts and average out how much you spend each month when you build your monthly budget. This can help you determine how much to budget for any expenses that may change from month to month.

Sticking to a Budget

Now you understand the finer points of budgeting. You've accomplished all of the above, even putting together a nice spreadsheet that lays out your budget for the next 15 years. The only problem is that sticking to that budget isn't as easy as you thought. That credit card still calls your name, your clothes category seems awfully small and you feel deprived. Budgets, you decide, are no fun. The good news is you don't have to throw it all out the window just because you've messed up once or twice.

Remember the Big Picture

The point of the budget is to keep you out of overwhelming debt and help you build a financial future that will give you more freedom, not less. So think about how you want your future to be and remember that keeping to your budget will help you get there. Adding to your debt load, on the other hand, will mean that your future could be even tighter.

Remove the Options That Allow You to Cheat on Your Budget

Make it more difficult for yourself to make impulse purchases. In other words, set up barriers so you have time to stop and think: "Is this purchase necessary?" Take yourself off retailer email lists. Remove your stored payment information on your favorite online shops so you can't just click to order.

Find Some Support

If you feel like you're the only one in your group who is on a budget, search and find some like-minded folks. It could be an online forum, a monthly meeting, or even just a couple of friends traveling the same budgetary road. You need to know you're not the only person setting sane financial limits for yourself. You can also have accountability with your frugal buddies, talking things over and each other out of temptation.

Go Old School

There's something powerful about handing over a stack of $20 bills for purchase: It causes you to really think about the amount of money you're about to spend. Swiping a debit card, on the other hand, may not feel nearly as real. Similarly, paying bills by writing checks and promptly entering the sums into your register keeps you up-to-date on how your account is affected in a way that autopay doesn't. You don't have to use cash exclusively or completely forgo online payments, but handling transactions in old-fashioned ways can make you realize how much you're spending and enhance the power of self-regulation.

Reward Yourself

If you constantly look at what you have to cut and give up, the very act of budgeting becomes distasteful. A mixture of long- and short-term gifts to yourself will help keep you motivated. When you've been faithful to your budget for a month, give yourself a reward. Even small ones can help, such as a night out with friends, a concert or a little extra cash for spending. Keep visual reminders of these rewards or the things you're saving up for. Start building associations in your brain—that sticking to your budget has a pleasurable result.

Schedule a Periodic Budget Evaluation

It's difficult to predict how much money you'll need in every category of life; a new job may necessitate a wardrobe change and your clothing budget may not cut it. That's why it's important to have a regular check on how you've created your budget. If it isn't working, tweak it. It is your budget, after all—just make sure you keep your long-term financial goals in the picture.

Educate Yourself

Instead of taking the more common road of instant gratification, which leads so easily to overspending and endless debt, learn all you can about finances, money management, and how you can best invest in yourself. Talk to your financially savvy friends and get real-world tips and advice from people who are doing well with their money. The more you learn about handling money wisely and its rewards, the more concrete the reasons for budgeting will be, and the better you will be at not only creating a budget that works for you, but also sticking to it.

Ways to Budget When You're Broke

Budgeting strategies sound fine, but if you're in dire straits financially or suffering from mounting bills and a lack of funds, there are some other possible steps to take.

1. Avoid Immediate Disaster

Don't be afraid to request bill extensions or payment plans from creditors. Skipping or delaying payments only worsens your debt—and besides, late fees ding your credit score.

2. Prioritize Bills

Go over all your bills to see what must be paid first and then set up a payment schedule based on your paydays. You will want to leave yourself some catch-up time if some of your bills are already late. If this is the case, call the bill companies to see how much you can pay now to get back on track toward positive status. Tell them you are taking strict measures to catch up. Be honest about the amount you can afford to pay; don't just promise to pay the full amount later.

3. Ignore the 10% Savings Rule

Stashing 10% of your income into your savings account is daunting when you're living paycheck to paycheck. It doesn't make sense to have $100 in a savings plan if you are fending off debt collectors. Your piggy bank will have to starve until you can find financial stability.

4. Review Spending

To fix your finances, you need to get a handle on your outlay first. Online banking and online budgeting software can help you categorize spending so you can make adjustments. Many people find that just by looking at aggregate figures for discretionary expenses, they are spurred to change their patterns and reduce excessive spending.

5. Eliminate Unnecessary Expenses

Once you've got a sense of where the money goes, it's time to tighten up. All cutbacks should start with items you wouldn't miss or habits you should change anyway—like reducing your fresh food purchases if you find ingredients spoiling before you can eat them. Or preparing meals at home more instead of going to restaurants or getting takeout. Some expenses you shouldn't drop but might be able to adjust could include reducing your auto insurance rate by switching carriers.

6. Negotiate Credit Card Interest Rates

There are other proactive ways to reduce expenses. Those killer interest rates on your credit cards aren't fixed in stone, for example. Call the card company and ask for a reduction in the annual percentage rates (APR). So if you have a good record, your request might be approved. This won't lower your outstanding balance, but it will keep it from mushrooming as fast.

7. Keep a Budget Journal

Once you've gone through these steps, monitor your progress for a few months. You can do this by writing everything you spend in a notebook, via budgeting apps on your phone, or with the software you used in step 4 to review your spending. How you track your money isn't as important as how much you are tracking. Focus on ensuring that every cent is accounted for by dividing your expenses into categories. Fine-tune and adjust the spending as needed after each month.

8. Seek New Income

For the time being, saving and investing money is out. But consider ways to increase earnings: working overtime, getting a second job, or picking up some freelance work. A budget isn't a prison cell to keep you away from your money. Rather, it's a tool you use to make sure your future is better—and yes, richer, than your present.

How Do You Create a Budget?

Creating a budget takes some work. You'll need to calculate every type of income you receive each month. Next, track your spending and tabulate all your monthly expenses, including your rent or mortgage, utility payments, debt, transportation costs, food, spending money, and others. And write it down. The only way to reinforce your budget is to see it in writing. You may have to make some adjustments initially just to stay within your budget. But once you've gone through the first few months, it should become easier to stick to it.

What Is the 50-20-30 Budget Rule?

The 50-20-30 budget rule was popularized by Sen. Elizabeth Warren (D-Mass.) in her book All Your Worth: The Ultimate Lifetime Money Plan. The plan entails dividing all of your after-tax income into 50% on your actual needs, 30% on anything you want, and 20% on savings.

How Does Budgeting Help a Business?

Just like budgets help people, corporate budgeting helps businesses stay on track. This way, they don't stray very far from what they've projected. They also help business leaders make very important (investment) decisions, manage and meet goals and objectives, and identify any hurdles that come their way.

The word budget often conjures up images of complicated financial documents. But it's a tool that can be used by various entities, including governments, businesses, and individuals/households of every income level. The key is to learn how to craft one and how to stick to it. Once you have these key points under your belt, you'll be better prepared at securing your financial future.

WHAT IS RETIREMENT PLANNING? STEPS, STAGES, AND WHAT TO CONSIDER

Retirement planning involves determining retirement income goals and what's needed to achieve those goals. Retirement planning includes identifying income sources, sizing up expenses, implementing a savings program, and managing assets and risk. Future cash flows are estimated to gauge whether the retirement income goal is possible. You can start at any time, but it works best if you factor it into your financial planning as early as possible. That's the best way to ensure a safe, secure—and fun—retirement. The fun part is why it makes sense to pay attention to the serious and perhaps boring part: planning how you'll get there.

8 Essential Tips For Retirement Saving

In the simplest sense, retirement planning is what one does to be prepared for life after paid work ends. This isn't just financially but in all aspects of life. The non-financial aspects include lifestyle choices such as how to spend time in retirement, where to live, and when to quit working altogether, among other things. A holistic approach to retirement planning considers all these areas. The emphasis that one puts on retirement planning changes at different stages of life. For instance:

Early in a person's working life, retirement planning is about setting aside enough money for retirement.

During the middle of your career, it might also include setting specific income or asset targets and taking steps to achieve them.

Once you reach retirement age, you go from accumulating assets to what planners call the distribution phase. You're no longer paying into your retirement account(s). Instead, your decades of saving begin paying you out.

Some retirement plans change depending on where you are. For instance, the United States and Canada each have unique systems of workplace-sponsored plans.

How Much Do You Need to Retire?

Remember that retirement planning starts long before you retire. The general rule is the sooner you start, the better. Your magic number, which is the amount you need to retire comfortably, is highly personalized. But there are numerous rules of thumb that can give you an idea of how much to save. How much you need depends on who you ask. For instance:

People used to say that you need around $1 million to retire comfortably.

Other professionals use the 80% rule, which states that you need enough to live on 80% of your income at retirement. So if you made $100,000 per year, then you would need savings that could produce $80,000 per year for roughly 20 years, or a total of $1.6 million, including the income generated by your retirement assets.

Others say most retirees aren't saving anywhere near enough to meet those benchmarks and should adjust their lifestyle to live on what they have.

While the amount of money you'll want to have in your nest egg is important, it's also a good idea to consider all of your expenses. Be sure to calculate the costs for housing, health insurance, food, clothing, and your vehicle/transportation. And since you'll have more free time on your hands, you may also want to factor in the cost of entertainment and travel. While it may be hard to come up with concrete figures, be sure to come up with a reasonable estimate so there are no surprises later on. Start as early as you can on whatever method that you, and possibly a financial planner, use to calculate your retirement savings needs.

Steps to Retirement Planning

Regardless of where you are in life, there are several key steps that apply to almost everyone during their retirement planning. The following are some of the most common:

Come up with a plan. This includes deciding when you want to start saving when you want to retire, and how much you'd like to save for your ultimate goal.

Decide how much you'll set aside each month. Using automatic deductions takes away the guesswork, keeps you on track, and takes away the temptation to stop or forget depositing money on your own.

Choose the right accounts for you. Take the chance to invest in a 401(k) or similar account if your employer offers that option. Remember, if the company offers an employer match and you don't sign up, you're just giving away free money. And don't forget to have an emergency fund, which can be easily liquidated if you need cash in a pinch.

Check on your investments from time to time and make periodic adjustments. It's always a good idea to make any changes whenever there's a change in your lifestyle and when you enter a different stage in your life.

Retirement Plans

Retirement accounts come in many shapes and sizes. The rules and regulations for each may be different.

Employer-Sponspored Plans

Young adults should take advantage of employer-sponsored 401(k) or 403(b) plans. The former is a type of retirement account offered by major corporations. The latter is a similar plan used by employees of public schools and certain charities. Both work in similar fashions. An up-front benefit of these qualified retirement plans is that your employer has the option to match what you invest up to a certain amount. For example, if you contribute 3% of your annual income to your plan account, your employer may match that and deposit the equivalent sum into your retirement account, essentially giving you a 3% bonus that grows over the years. You can and should contribute more than the amount that will earn the employer match. In fact, some experts recommend upward of 10%. For the 2023 tax year, participants under age 50 can contribute up to $22,500 of their earnings to a 401(k) or 403(b) (up from $20,500 for 2022), some of which may be additionally matched by an employer. People over age 50 can contribute an extra $7,500 per year as a catch-up contribution (up from $6,500 in 2022). Additional advantages of 401(k) plans include earning a higher rate of return than a savings account (although the investments are not free of risk). Also, the funds within the account are not subject to income tax until you withdraw them. Since your contributions are taken off your gross income, you will get an immediate income tax break. Those who are on the cusp of a higher tax bracket might consider contributing enough to lower their tax liability.

Traditional Individual Retirement Account (IRA)
The traditional individual retirement account (IRA) lets you put aside pre-tax dollars. This means that the money you save is deducted from your income before your taxes are taken out. As such, it lowers your taxable income and, therefore, your tax liability. So if you're on the cusp of a higher tax bracket, investing in a traditional IRA can knock you down to a lower one. The tax benefit to this kind of account is upfront. So when it comes time to take distributions from the account, you are subject to your

standard tax rate at that time. Keep in mind, though, that the money grows on a tax-deferred basis. There are no capital gains or dividend taxes that are assessed on the balance of your account until you begin making withdrawals. The IRS sets limits on how much you can contribute to a traditional IRA each year. This figure is set based on inflation. The limit for 2023 is $6,500 (up from $6,000 in 2022). People who are 50 and older can invest an additional $1,000 for a total of $7,500 in 2023 (up from $6,500 in 2022).

Distributions must be taken at age 72 and can be taken as early as 59½. You are subject to a 10% penalty if you make withdrawals before that. You will also incur taxes at your regular income tax rate.

Roth Individual Retirement Account (IRA)

A Roth IRA can be an excellent tool for young adults, funded with post-tax dollars. This eliminates the immediate tax deduction but avoids a more significant income tax bite when the money is withdrawn at retirement. Starting a Roth IRA early can pay off big time in the long run, even if you don't have a lot of money to invest at first. Remember, the longer the money sits in a retirement account, the more tax-free interest is earned.

Roth IRAs have some limitations. The contribution limit for either IRA (Roth or traditional) is $6,500 a year, or $7,500 if you are over age 50. Still, a Roth has some income limits: A single filer can contribute the full amount only if they make $129,000 or less annually, as of the 2022 tax year, and $138,000 in 2023. After that, you can invest to a lesser degree, up to an annual income of $144,000 in 2022 and $153,000 in 2023. (The income limits are higher for married couples filing jointly.) Like a 401(k), a Roth IRA has some penalties associated with taking money out before you hit retirement age. But there are a few notable exceptions that may be very useful for younger people or in case of emergency. First, you can always withdraw the initial capital you invested without paying a penalty. Second, you can withdraw funds for certain educational expenses, a first-time home purchase, health care expenses, and disability costs.

SIMPLE Individual Retirement Account (IRA)

The SIMPLE IRA is a retirement account offered to employees of small businesses in lieu of the 401(k), which is expensive to maintain. It works the same way a 401(k) does, allowing employees to save money automatically through payroll deductions with the option of an employer match. This amount is capped at 3% of an employee's annual salary. The annual contribution limit for a SIMPLE IRA is $15,500 in 2023, up from $14,000 in 2022. Catch-up contributions of $3,500 allow employees 50 or older to bump that limit up to $19,000.

Once you set up a retirement account, the question becomes how to direct the funds. For those intimidated by the stock market, consider investing in an index fund that requires little maintenance, as it simply mirrors a stock market index like the Standard & Poor's 500. Target-date funds are also designed to automatically alter and diversify assets over time based on your goal retirement age.

Stages of Retirement Planning

Below are some guidelines for successful retirement planning at different stages of your life.

Young Adulthood (Ages 21–35)

Those embarking on adult life may not have a lot of money free to invest, but they do have time to let investments mature, which is a critical and valuable piece of retirement savings. This is because of the principle of compounding. Compound interest allows interest to earn interest, and the more time you have, the more interest you will earn. Even if you can only put aside $50 a month, it will be worth three times more if you invest it at age 25 than if you wait to start investing until age 45, thanks to the joys of compounding. You might be able to invest more money in the future, but you'll never be able to make up for any lost time. Keep in mind that certain federal agencies and uniformed services offer thrift savings plans.

Early Midlife (Ages 36–50)

Early midlife tends to bring a number of financial strains, including mortgages, student loans, insurance premiums, and credit card debt. However, it's critical to continue saving at this stage of retirement planning. The combination of earning more money and the time you still have to invest and earn interest makes these years some of the best for aggressive savings. People at this stage of retirement planning should continue to take advantage of any 401(k) matching programs that their employers offer. They should also try to max out contributions to a 401(k) or Roth IRA (you can have both at the same time). For those ineligible for a Roth IRA, consider a traditional IRA. As with your 401(k), this is funded with pretax dollars, and the assets within it grow tax-deferred. Some employer-sponsored plans offer a Roth option to set aside after-tax retirement contributions. You are limited to the same annual limit, but there are no income limitations as with a Roth IRA.

Finally, don't neglect life insurance and disability insurance. You want to ensure that your family could survive financially without pulling from retirement savings should something happen to you.

Later Midlife (Ages 50–65)

As you age, your investment accounts should become more conservative. Treasury bills (T-bills) are one of the most conservative investments, but their returns are also low compared to other investments. While time is running out to save for people at this stage of retirement planning, there are a few advantages. Higher wages and potentially having some of the aforementioned expenses (mortgages, student loans, credit card debt, etc.) paid off by this time can leave you with more disposable income to invest. And it's never too late to set up and contribute to a 401(k) or an IRA. One benefit of this retirement planning stage is catch-up contributions. From age 50 on, you can contribute an additional $1,000 a year to your traditional or Roth IRA and an additional $7,500 a year to your 401(k) in 2023 (up from $6,500 for 2022). For those who have maxed out tax-incentivized retirement savings options, consider other forms of investment to supplement your retirement savings. Certificates of deposit (CDs), blue-chip stocks, or certain real estate investments (like a vacation home that you rent out) may be reasonably safe ways to add to your nest egg.

You can also begin to get a sense of what your Social Security benefits will be and at what age it makes sense to start taking them. Eligibility for early benefits starts at age 62, but the retirement age for full benefits is 66. This is also the time to look into long-term care insurance, which will help cover the costs of a nursing home or home care should you need it in your advanced years. If you don't properly plan for health-related expenses, especially unexpected ones, they can decimate your savings.

Other Aspects of Retirement Planning

Retirement planning includes a lot more than simply how much you will save and how much you need. It takes into account your complete financial picture.

Your Home

For most Americans, the single biggest asset they own is their home. How does that fit into your retirement plan? A home was considered an asset in the past, but since the housing market crash, planners see it as less of an asset than they once did. With the popularity of home equity loans and home equity lines of credit (HELOCs), many homeowners are entering retirement in mortgage debt instead of well above water. Once you retire, there's also the question of whether you should sell your home. If you still live in the home where you raised multiple children, it might be more significant than you need, and the expenses that come with holding onto it might be considerable. Your retirement plan should include an unbiased look at your home and what to do with it.

Estate Planning

Your estate plan addresses what happens to your assets after you die. It should include a will that lays out your plans, but even before that, you should set up a trust or use some other strategy to keep as much of it as possible shielded from estate taxes. As of 2023, the first $12.92 million of an estate is exempt from estate taxes (up from $12.06 million for 2022), but more and more people are finding ways to leave their money to their children in a way that doesn't pay them in a lump sum. There may also be changes coming down the pipeline in Congress regarding estate taxes, as the estate tax amount is scheduled to drop to $5 million in 2026.

Tax Efficiency

Once you reach retirement age and begin taking distributions, taxes become a big problem. Most of your retirement accounts are taxed as ordinary income tax. That means you could pay as much as 37% in taxes on any money that you take from your traditional 401(k) or IRA. That's why it's essential to consider a Roth IRA or a Roth 401(k), as both allow you to pay taxes upfront rather than upon withdrawal. If you believe you will make more money later in life, it may make sense to do a Roth conversion. An accountant or financial planner can help you work through such tax considerations.

Insurance

A key component of retirement planning is protecting your assets. Age comes with increased medical expenses, and you will have to navigate the often-complicated Medicare system. Many people feel that standard Medicare doesn't provide adequate coverage, so they look to a Medicare Advantage or Medigap policy to supplement it. There's also life insurance and long-term care insurance to consider. Another type of policy issued by an insurance company is an annuity. An annuity is much like a pension. You put money on deposit with an insurance company that later pays you a set monthly amount. There are many different options with annuities and many considerations when deciding if an annuity is right for you.

How Do I Start Planning for Retirement?

Retirement planning isn't difficult. It's as easy as setting aside some money every month—every little bit counts. The easiest way is to start contributing through an employer-sponsored plan if your company offers one. You may also want to consider talking to a professional, such as a financial planner or investment broker who can steer you in the right direction. The earlier you start, the better. That's because your investments grow over time by earning interest. And you'll earn interest on that interest.

Why Is Retirement Planning So Important?

Retirement planning allows you to sock away enough money to maintain the same lifestyle you currently have. After all, no one wants to work right up until the end. While you may work part-time or pick up the odd gig here or there, it probably won't be enough to sustain your current lifestyle. And Social Security benefits will only take you so far. That's why it's so important to have a viable plan that allows you to get the maximum amount of money when you retire.

What Other Aspects Should I Consider During Retirement?

Retirement planning is such an important part of your financial well-being. But there are other things you need to consider outside of what happens after you retire. Ensure that your finances are giving you the biggest tax breaks possible, so a Roth conversion may be a good idea if you believe you'll be earning some income later on in life. You may also want to consider what happens to your assets after you die, which is where estate planning comes into play. Life insurance can help offset any expenses that you leave behind for your loved ones if you become injured or die unexpectedly.

Everyone dreams of the day they can finally say goodbye to the workforce and retire. But doing so costs money. That's where retirement planning comes into play. And it doesn't matter at which point you are in your life. Sure, you may have Social Security benefits, but that may not be enough, especially if you're used to a certain lifestyle. Setting aside money now means you'll have less to worry about later.

Top Financial Tips for Teens

Use Time Wisely

If you're not making a lot of money, it doesn't matter. What matters is time, and your money will have a lot of it because you're young. For example, if you have a summer job and at the end of it you saved $1,000, you save that money a variety of ways, including:

Opening a savings account or open one with your parents so that you receive a higher interest rate.

Giving a portion of your money to your parents to invest in a business, stocks, bonds, or real estate.

Save your money at home, add to it, and then invest it.

If you invest your $1,000 at a rate of return of 5% and don't do anything else for 50 years, you will have $11,467.49. At the end of 30 years, you would have $4,321.99. Imagine how fast your money will grow if you start saving very early. Time is on your side right now so take advantage of it.

Get into the Habit of Saving

We've touched on saving in the first point, but it begs to repeat. If your parents saved your birthday or holiday money since your birth, you're off to a great start. Keep the momentum going by saving any money given to you by your grandparents, parents, and other relatives. When you get older, you could do things around your neighborhood, such as shoveling snow, babysitting, or mowing lawns. Save the money you receive because it will add up over time.

Create a Budget

It's a good idea to have a teenage financial budget. Why? Because as you get older, you may prefer paying for certain items such as makeup, clothing, and bath and body. Keep in mind that a budget for high school students may have more expenses. For instance, if you have a car, you'll have to budget for gas, insurance, and repairs. However, your parents may help pay for the latter. You want your income to exceed your expenses. If it doesn't see where you can save decrease your expenses.

Track and Lower Your Expenses

Our Club Ignite is exclusively for teens and can help you track your expenses because you'll receive a Club Ignite card. Not only can you make deposits at the ATM, but when you swipe your debit card, you can track your spending. It's a great way to manage your money. And if you notice your balance getting low, it means you're spending too much and time to save more money.

Establish a Credit History

Your parents can help you establish a credit history before you go out on your own, which is better than dropping you off at college, handing you a credit card, which essentially says, "Good luck. Go be responsible." Ask your parents to add you as an authorized user on a credit card. They don't have to give you access to it. However, adding you to the account opens a credit file in your name. Once this happens, you'll want to check and understand what makes up a credit score.

Think Carefully about College

With student loan debt on the rise, you may want to delay college or opt for community college since the tuition costs less than a four-year university. If you know that you want to go to college, open a College Savings Account so that you can save money for school. You can also apply for grants and scholarships and inquire about paid internships.

Take Advantage of Your Student ID

Did you know that your student ID could help you get up to 10 percent off at retailers such as Levis, Apple, and other retailers? Think about how much you can save because of discounted prices. Keep in mind that some businesses may not promote student discounts, but all you have to do is ask!

Get a Summer Job or Start an Online Business

You could get a summer job or ask your parents to help you start an online business. For example, if you like to bake cupcakes and other sweet treats, you could open an online bakery business. Ask your friends and siblings to help you with making deliveries. Or maybe you could be a camp counselor or tutor summer school students. Think about what you love to do, a hobby perhaps, and get help turning it into a business.

CONCLUSION

You may ask yourself, "What should I save up for as a teenager?" If you want a big-ticket item such as an iPhone or something else, you'll need to cover the initial cost and any other expenses. Only you know if something is worth it or not. Being a smart money manager means that you can delay instant gratification so that you can build your savings. It may not be easy, but when your bank account grows and grows, you may have enough funds to pay for something really special and still have money left over.